monday
morning®

CENTERS for COLORS & SHAPES

by Marilynn G. Barr

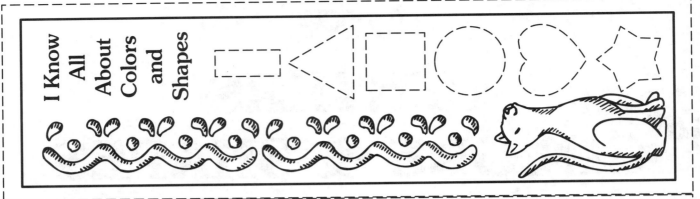

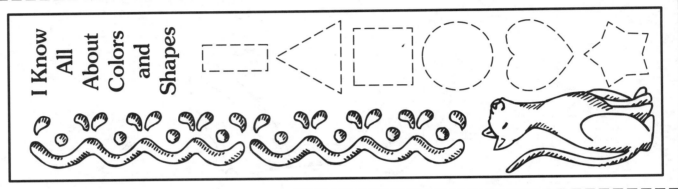

Publisher: Monday Morning Books, Inc.

Production: Little Acorn & Associates, Inc.

MM2224
CENTERS FOR COLORS & SHAPES
Entire contents copyright © 2007
by Monday Morning Books, Inc.

For a complete catalog, write to the address below:
Monday Morning Books, Inc.
PO Box 1134
Inverness, CA 94937

Call our toll-free number: 1-800-255-6049
E-mail us at: MMBooks@aol.com
Visit our Web site: http://www.mondaymorningbooks.com
For more products featuring art by Marilynn G. Barr visit www.littleacornbooks.com

monday Morning®

ISBN 1-57612-228-X

Printed in the United States of America
9 8 7 6 5 4 3 2 1

Contents

Introduction

Centers for Colors & Shapes offers children lots of circus-theme skills practice. Children practice sorting and matching plain and patterned shapes, color words, and objects. Youngsters also practice fine motor skills as they attach clothespins to match boards; trace, color, and draw shapes; and cut out and glue puppet patterns to craft sticks. Each center includes five practice stations: Match It, Trace It, Write It (Color It or Draw It), Read It, and Review It. While very early learners may require some guidance as they move from station to station, each activity is designed for self-directed skills practice.

Setting Up Centers

Below is a list of supplies and storage formats to set up each five-station center for children to practice matching, tracing, writing, reading, and reviewing. Set up an additional "Make It" station for children to make stick puppets. Children can work individually or in small groups.

Supplies:

Construction paper, oak tag, crayons, glue, markers, scissors, file folders, craft sticks, clothespins, loose leaf binders, wipe-off crayons, paper plates (optional), baskets, file boxes

Folders:

Decorate folders to store Trace It and Write It activities as well as mini book pages and Review It activities.

Binders:

Fill binders with laminated activity sheets to keep in each station. Trace It, Write It, and the Color or Shape of the Day Flip Chart pages are designed with three holes to punch and place in loose leaf binders.

Reproduce, color, cut out, and tape or glue the Color or Shape of the Day Flip Chart cover to the front of a binder. Decorate oak tag covers for separate Trace It and Write It activity binders.

Assembling Activities

Match It

Reproduce, color, and cut out plain paper, oak tag, or poster board match boards. Laminate or glue plain paper match boards to paper plates for stability. Reproduce, color, cut out, and glue clothespins to the backs of matching cutouts.

Children clip clothespins to matching spaces around the match boards. Store Match It activities in separate resealable plastic bags. Place the bags in a basket in the designated Match It station.

Trace It

• Reproduce and place a supply of Trace It activity sheets in separate folders. Place a basket of crayons at the Trace It station for children to practice tracing. Store the folders in a file box decorated with puppet cutouts.

• Trace It Binder: Decorate and glue or tape a cover to the front of a binder to hold laminated Trace It activity sheets. Reproduce, color, laminate, and place Trace It activity sheets in the binder for children to practice tracing. Store wipe-off crayons in a loose leaf pencil pocket in the binder.

Write It, Color It, or Draw It

• Reproduce and place a supply of activity sheets in separate folders. Place a basket of crayons at a Write It, Color It, or Draw It station for children to practice writing, drawing, and coloring. Store the folders in a file box decorated with puppet cutouts.

• Write It, Color It, or Draw It Binder: Decorate and glue or tape a cover to the front of a binder to hold Write It activity sheets. Reproduce, color, laminate, and place Write It activity sheets in the binder for children to practice writing, coloring, and drawing. Store wipe-off crayons in a loose leaf pencil pocket in the binder.

Read It

Use mini book pages to make supersized and mini books for children to practice reading and learning about colors and shapes.

• Supersized Book: Enlarge, reproduce, color, and cut out each two-page mini book. Decorate a construction paper cover for each book. (Page one of each book can be used as a cover.)

• Make and Read It: Reproduce and staple several sets of mini book pages. Place like sets in separate folders in a decorated file box in the Read It station.

Help early learners color, cut out, and assemble book pages. Place pre-cut sheets of construction paper in a basket for children to decorate covers for their mini books. Write each child's name on the back of his or her assembled book.

Review It

Reproduce, color, and cut out each set of Review It patterns and cutouts. Matching in the center, glue each set of patterns inside a file folder. Decorate the front of the folder. Laminate the folder. Tape a construction paper pocket or an envelope to the back of each folder to store matching cutouts.

Store Review It folders in a file box in the designated station.

Puppets

Reproduce and cut out puppet patterns. Place the patterns in a basket with crayons for children to color and decorate. Help children glue craft sticks to the backs of cutouts to form stick puppets. Write each child's initials on his or her puppet.

Labels

Reproduce, color, and cut out the labels. Program and tape the labels on storage envelopes, boxes, folders, file boxes, or baskets.

Color or Shape of the Day Flip Chart

Introduce a new concept with a flip chart. Reproduce, color, cut out, and tape or glue the flip chart cover to the front of a loose leaf binder. Reproduce, color, and cut out several flip chart pages. Punch a hole at each dot on each page. Draw or color a shape, write a color word, or write a shape word on each page and place it in the binder. Pages can also be programmed with magazine cutouts featuring shapes or colors.

Borders

Children can practice identifying colors and shapes on the drum borders. Reproduce, color, and cut out the border patterns. Use the borders to decorate display boards, create frames, decorate folders and binders, or make headbands.

Monkeys on the High Wire

Reproduce and color each unicycle wheel a different color (red, yellow, blue, green, orange, purple). Cut out the match board.

6

Monkeys on the High Wire

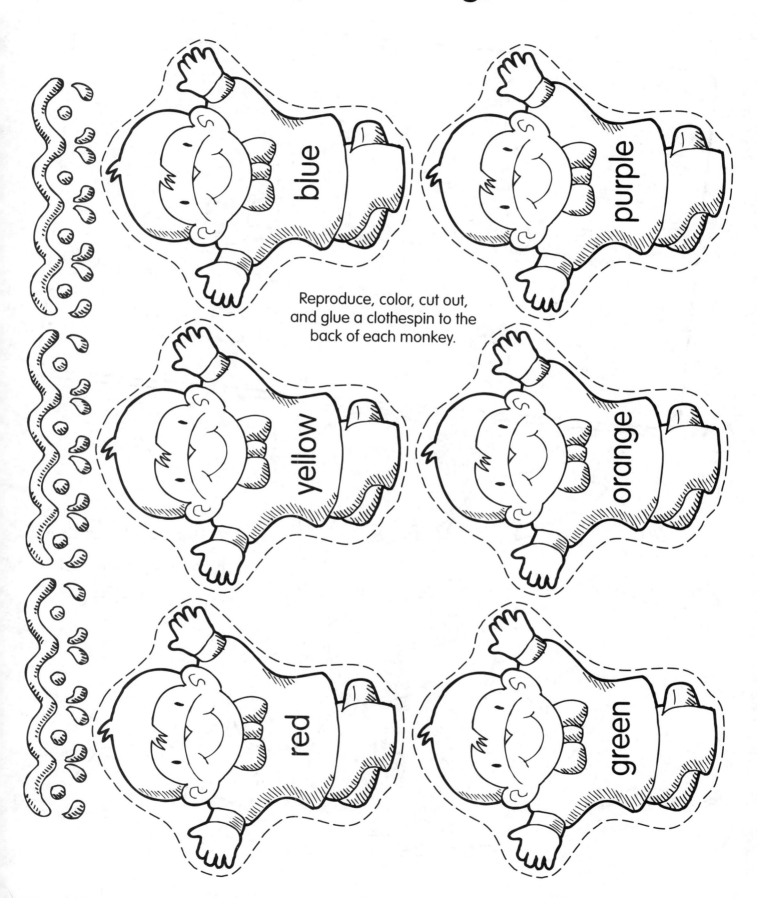

blue

purple

Reproduce, color, cut out, and glue a clothespin to the back of each monkey.

yellow

orange

red

green

Monkey's Balancing Act

red   green

yellow   orange

blue   purple

Trace the color words.
Color the stars to match.
Color the rest of the
picture.

Monkey Acrobats

Look at the color word in each block.
Color the blocks to match.
Color the rest of the picture.

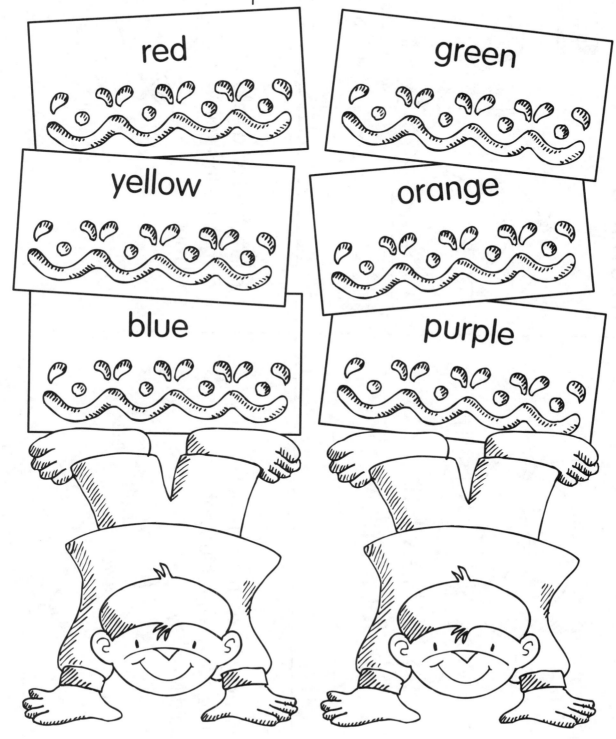

2

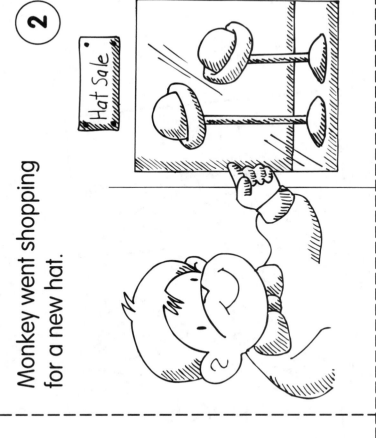

Monkey went shopping for a new hat.

4

Monkey tried on a yellow hat. "I do not like this yellow hat," said Monkey.

1

A New Hat for Monkey

3

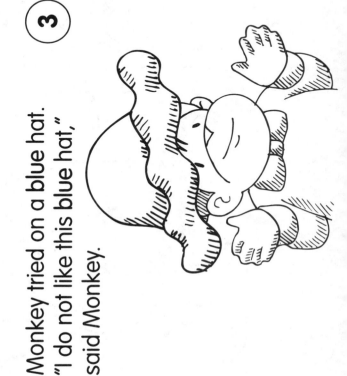

Monkey tried on a blue hat. "I do not like this blue hat," said Monkey.

A New Hat for Monkey

6

Monkey tried on an orange hat.
"I do not like this orange hat,"
said Monkey.

8

Monkey tried on a red hat.
"I like this red hat,"
said Monkey.

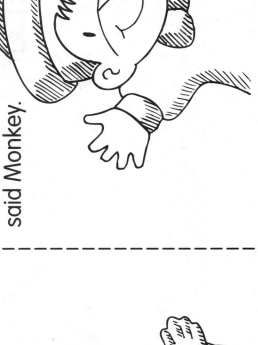

5

Monkey tried on a green hat.
"I do not like this green hat,"
said Monkey.

7

Monkey tried on a purple hat.
"I do not like this purple hat,"
said Monkey.

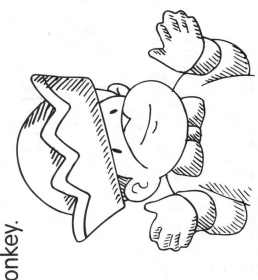

Monkey's Hoop Match

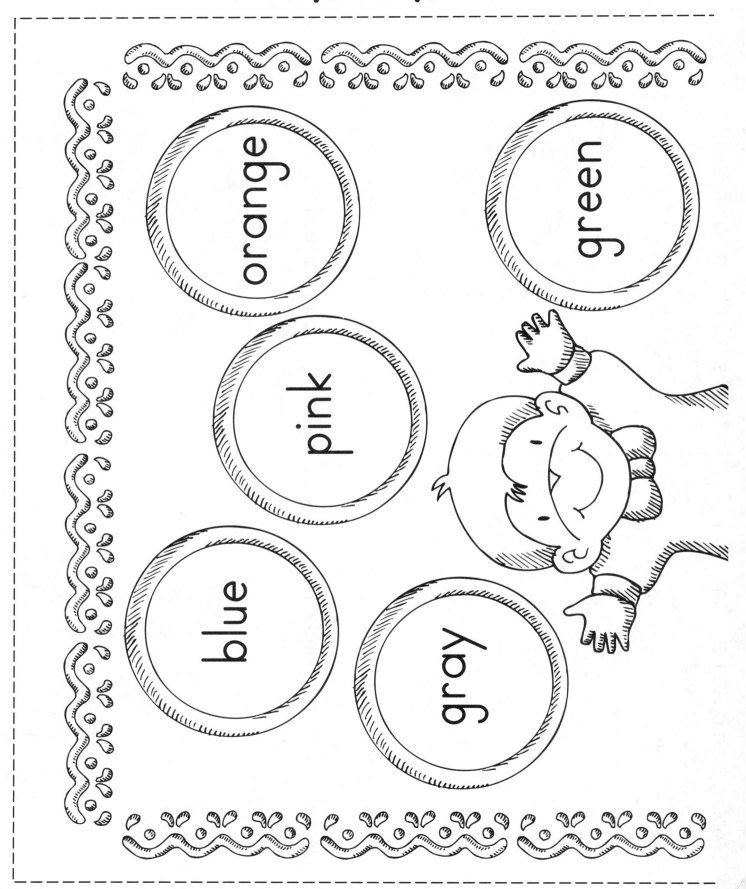

Monkey's Hoop Match

red

black

yellow

purple

brown

Place a matching hoop on each color word hoop.

Monkey's Hoop Match

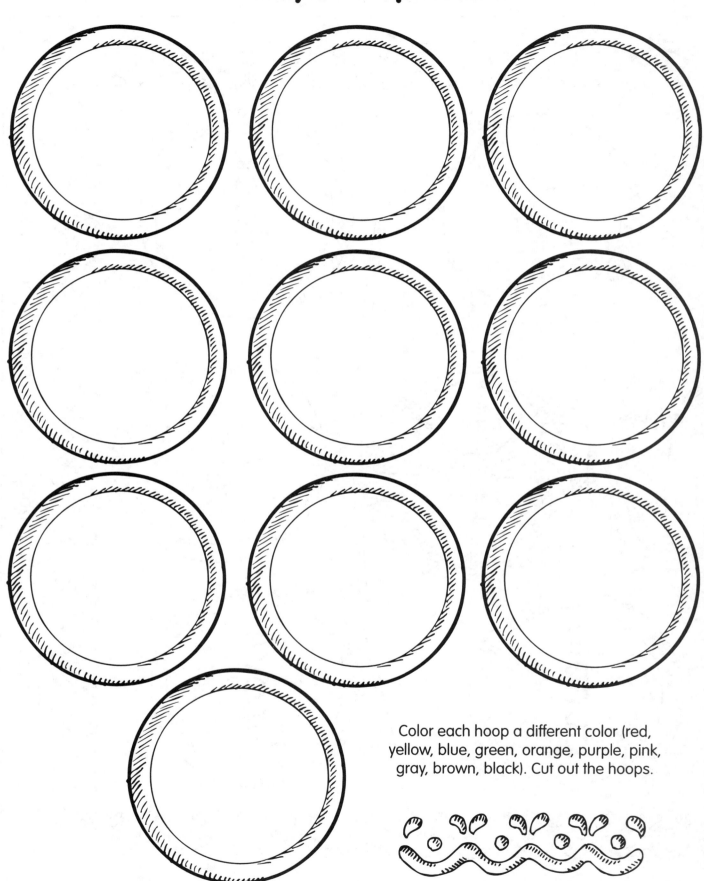

Color each hoop a different color (red, yellow, blue, green, orange, purple, pink, gray, brown, black). Cut out the hoops.

Monkey Puppets

Reproduce and color each monkey a different color (red, yellow, blue, green, orange, purple). Cut out the monkey patterns. Glue a craft stick to the back of each monkey to form a puppet.

Note: Reproduce a second set of monkey patterns for these additional colors (gray, pink, black, turquoise, brown, white).

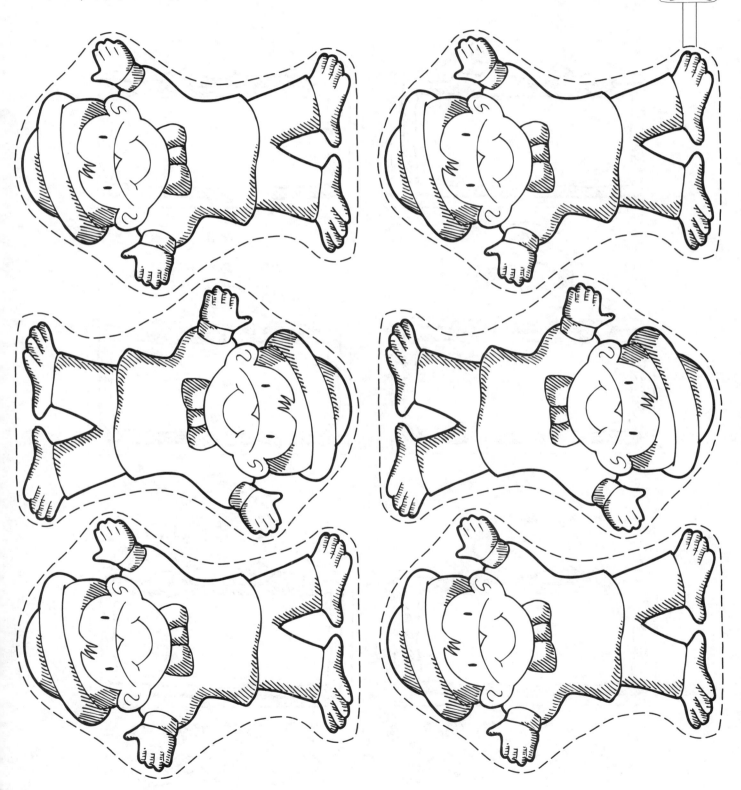

15

Monkey Labels

Reproduce, color, and cut out the labels.
Program and tape the labels on storage envelopes, boxes, folders, or drawers.

Horse and Saddles

Reproduce, color, and cut out the match board.

Horse and Saddles

Reproduce and color each saddle a different color (red, yellow, blue, green, orange, and purple).
Cut out and glue a clothespin to the back of each saddle.

A Dancing Horse

Trace the color words.
Color the blocks to match.
Color the rest of the picture.

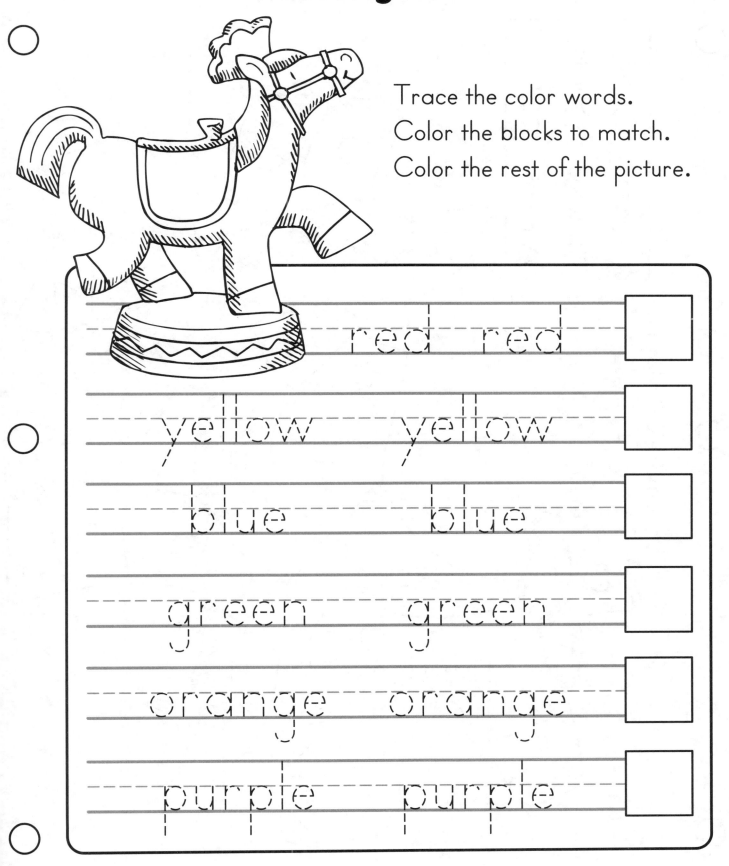

red red

yellow yellow

blue blue

green green

orange orange

purple purple

A Horse of a Different Color

Color It

Look at the color legend.
Color the horse.

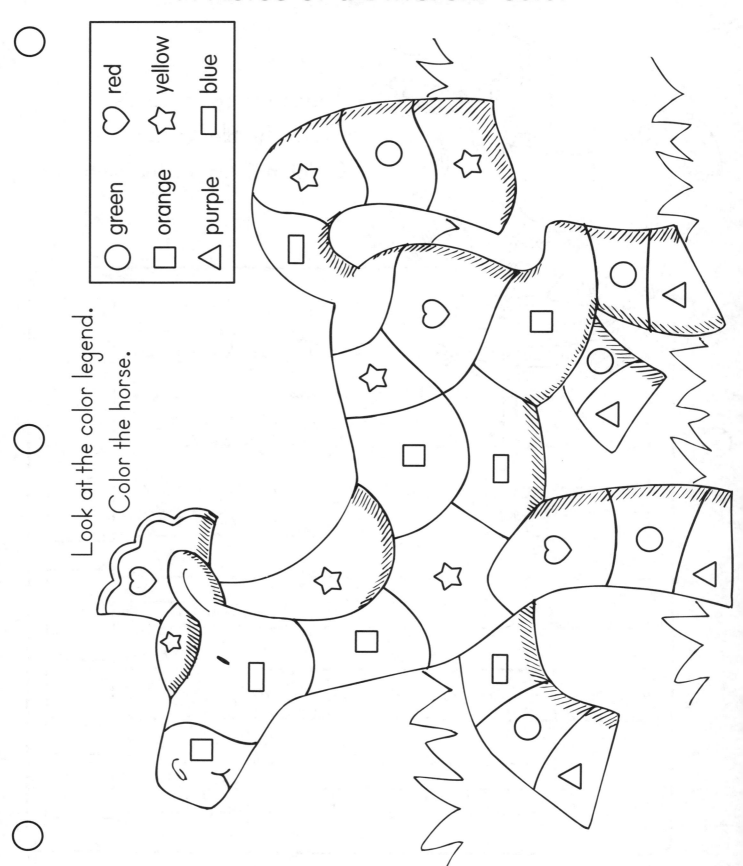

20

I See Rainbow Horses

② I see a red horse walking to the right.

④ I see a yellow horse sleeping.

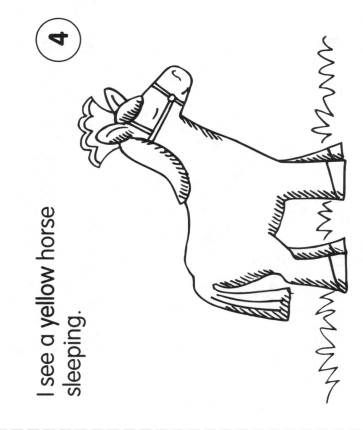

① I See Rainbow Horses

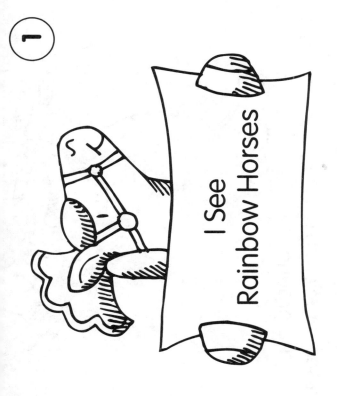

③ I see a blue horse walking to the left.

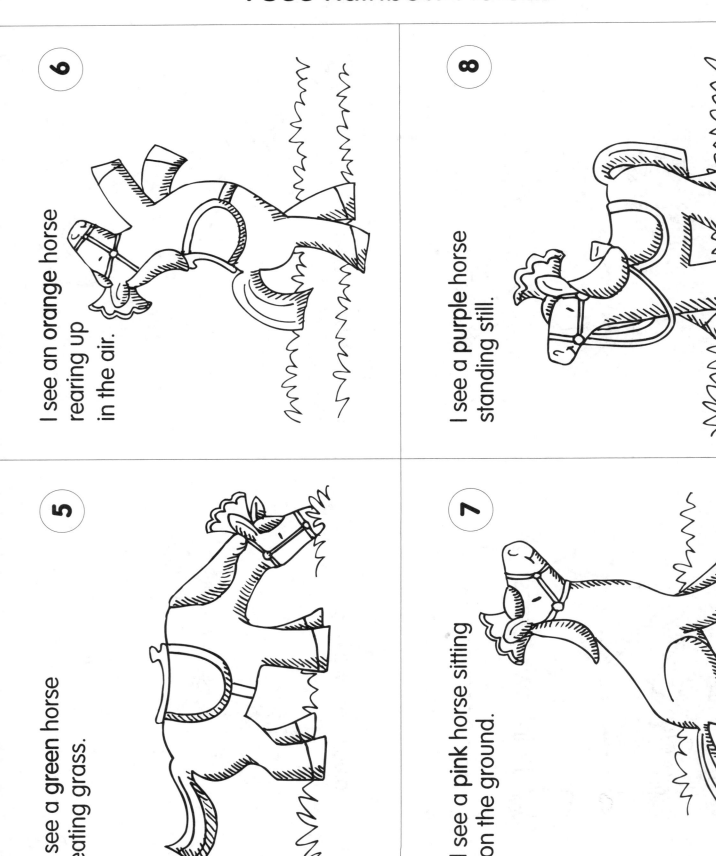

6

I see an orange horse rearing up in the air.

8

I see a purple horse standing still.

5

I see a green horse eating grass.

7

I see a pink horse sitting on the ground.

A Patchwork Horse

Place a matching patch on each color word patch.

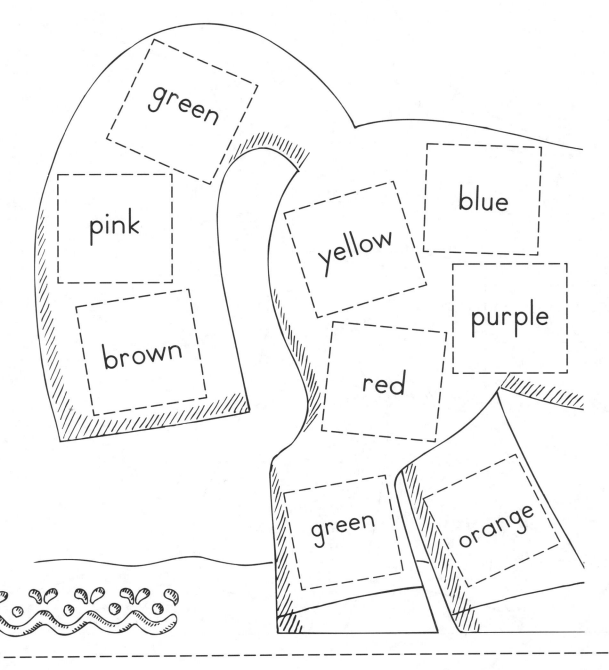

23

A Patchwork Horse

A Patchwork Horse

Reproduce, color, and cut out the patches (red, yellow, blue, green, orange, purple, pink, brown).

25

Horse Puppets

Reproduce and color each horse a different color (red, yellow, blue, green, orange, purple).
Cut out the horse patterns. Glue a craft stick to the back of each horse to form a puppet.

Note: Reproduce a second set of horse patterns for these additional colors
(gray, pink, black, turquoise, brown, white).

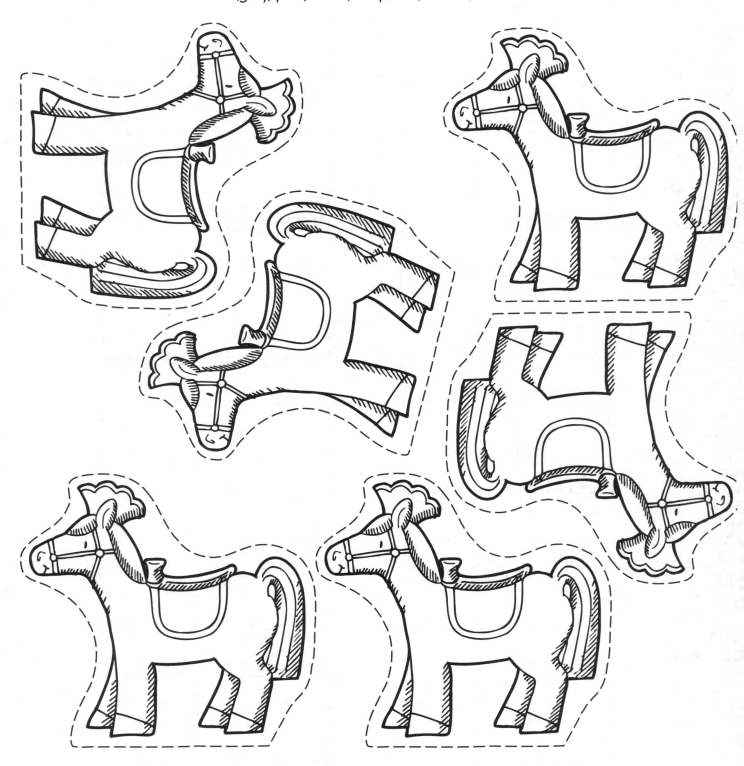

Horse Labels

Reproduce, color, and cut out the labels.
Program and tape the labels on storage envelopes, boxes, folders, or drawers.

Meet the Circus Bear Band

Reproduce, color, and cut out the match board.

Meet the Circus Bear Band

Reproduce, color, cut out, and glue a clothespin to the back of each instrument
(red, yellow, blue, green, orange, purple).

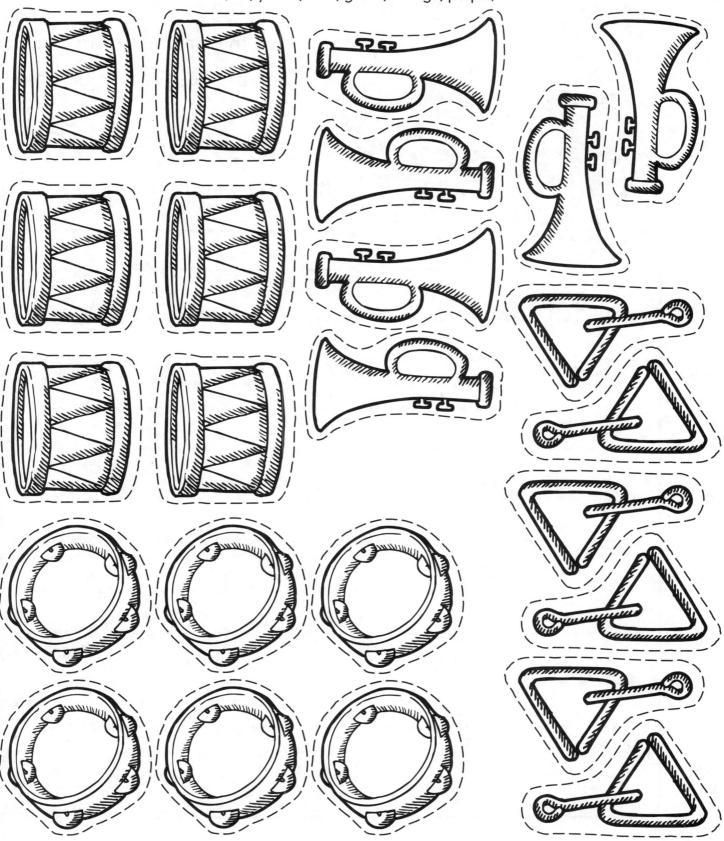

           ©2007 Monday Morning Books, Inc.

Drummer Bears

Trace the color words.
Color the drums to match.
Color the rest of the picture.

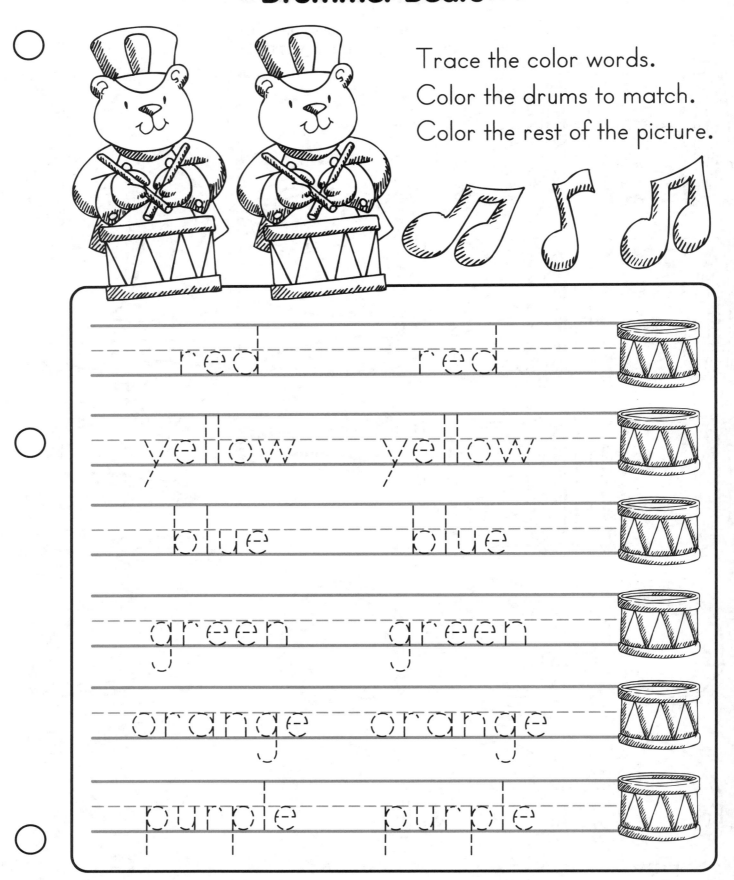

red   red

yellow   yellow

blue   blue

green   green

orange   orange

purple   purple

30

Colorful Notes

Look at each color word.
Write each color word.
Color the notes to match.
Color the rest of the picture.

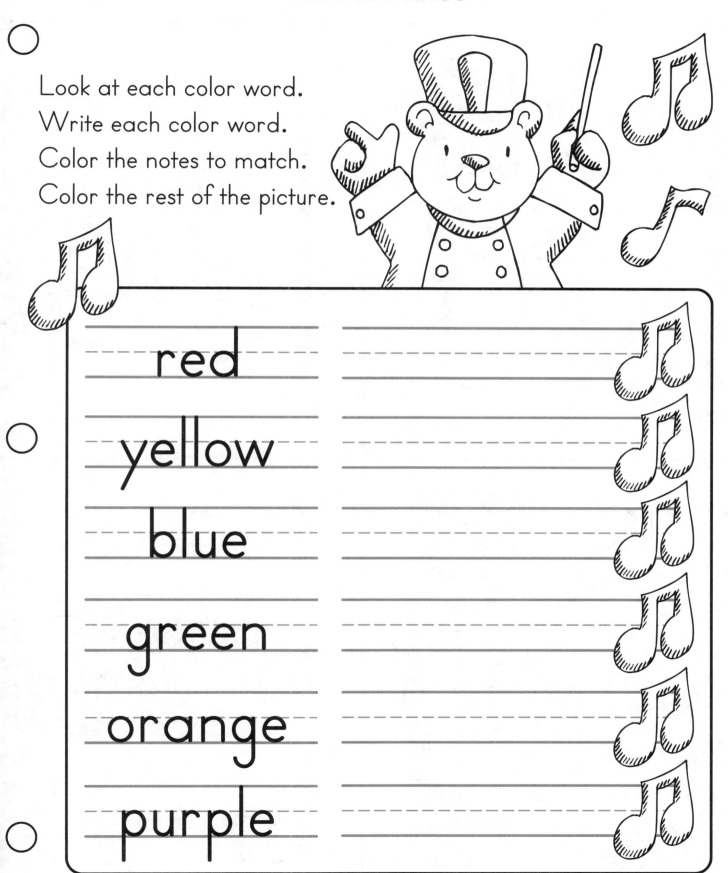

red

yellow

blue

green

orange

purple

31

Leader of the Band

② Who is the Leader of the Band?

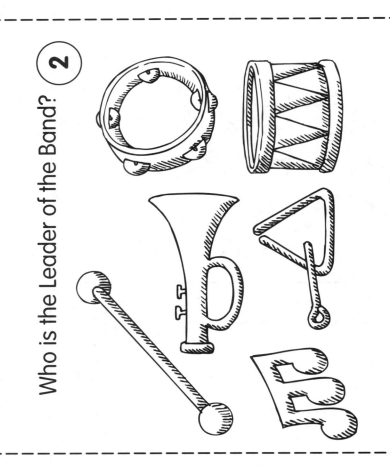

④ Purple Bear blows the horn.

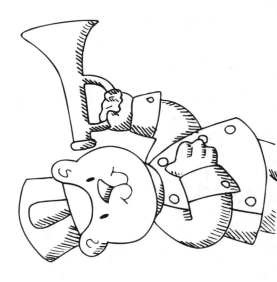

①

Leader of the Band

③ Green Bear bangs the drum.

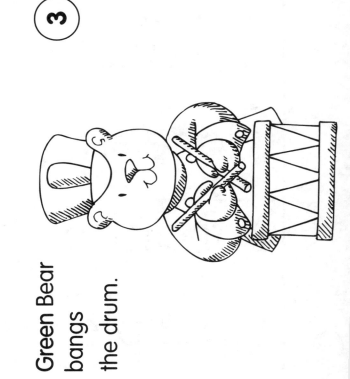

6 Orange Bear strikes the triangle.

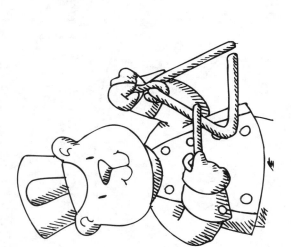

8 Red Bear is the leader of the band.

5 Brown Bear twirls the baton.

7 Blue Bear shakes the tambourine.

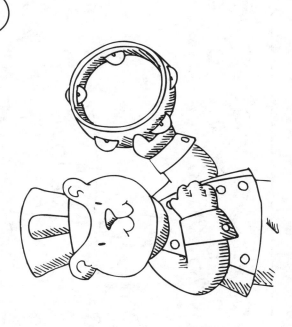

Uniforms for Bears

Uniforms for Bears

Place matching uniform patterns on each bear.

red

yellow

red

green

orange

green

Uniforms for Bears

Reproduce two sets of uniform patterns. Color each set a different color (red, yellow, blue, green, orange, purple). Cut out the patterns.

36

Bear Puppets

Reproduce and color each bear a different color (red, yellow, blue, green, orange, purple). Cut out the bear patterns. Glue a craft stick to the back of each bear to form a puppet.

Note: Reproduce a second set of bear patterns for these additional colors (gray, pink, black, turquoise, brown, white).

Bear Labels

Reproduce, color, and cut out the labels.
Program and tape the labels
on storage envelopes, boxes,
folders, or drawers.

Circus Dogs on Parade

Reproduce and color each stand a different color (red, yellow, blue, green, orange, purple). Cut out the match board.

39

Circus Dogs on Parade

Reproduce, cut out, and glue a clothespin to the back of each dog. Do not color the dogs.

40

Fancy Capes

Trace the dotted lines on each dog. Color the picture.

41

Fancy Hats

○ Look at the color legend. Color the hats. Color the picture.

red

yellow

blue

green

orange

purple

pink

brown

42

A New House for Circus Dog

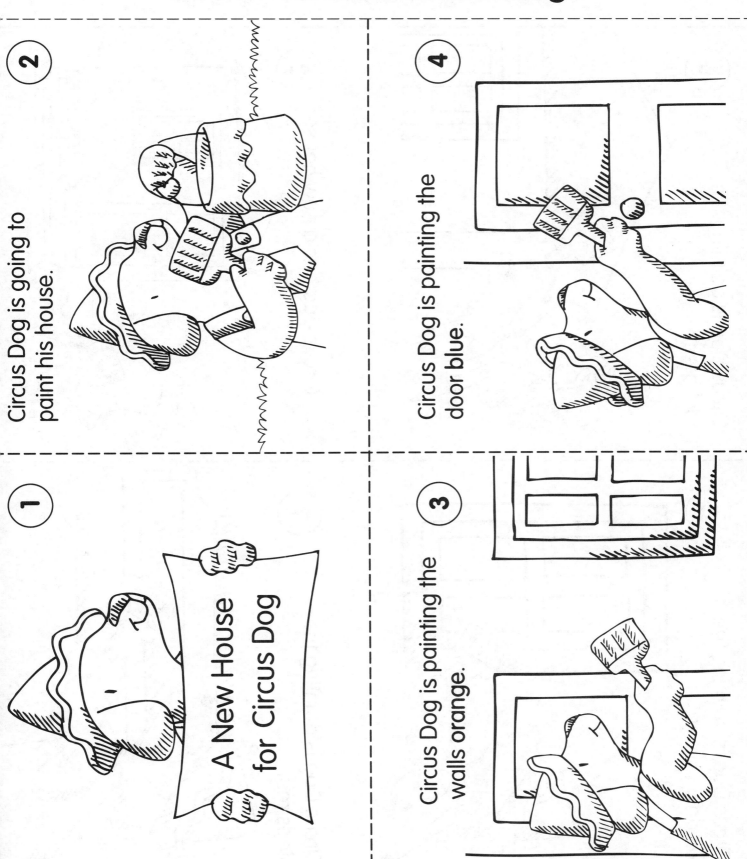

2 Circus Dog is going to paint his house.

4 Circus Dog is painting the door blue.

1 A New House for Circus Dog

3 Circus Dog is painting the walls orange.

43

A New House for Circus Dog

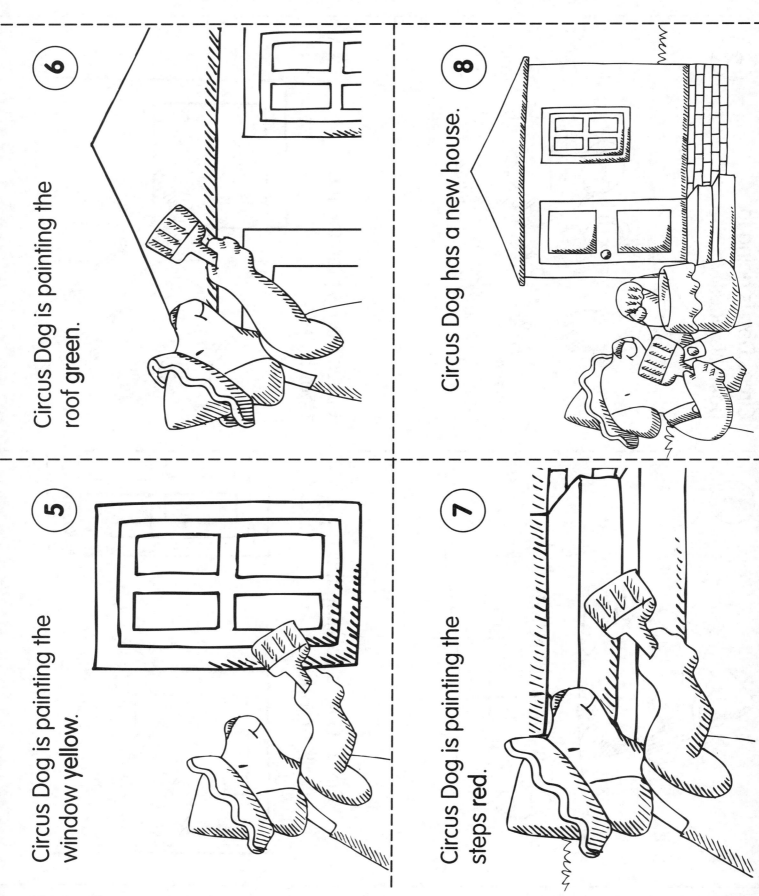

6 Circus Dog is painting the roof green.

8 Circus Dog has a new house.

5 Circus Dog is painting the window yellow.

7 Circus Dog is painting the steps red.

Circus Dogs Dress Up

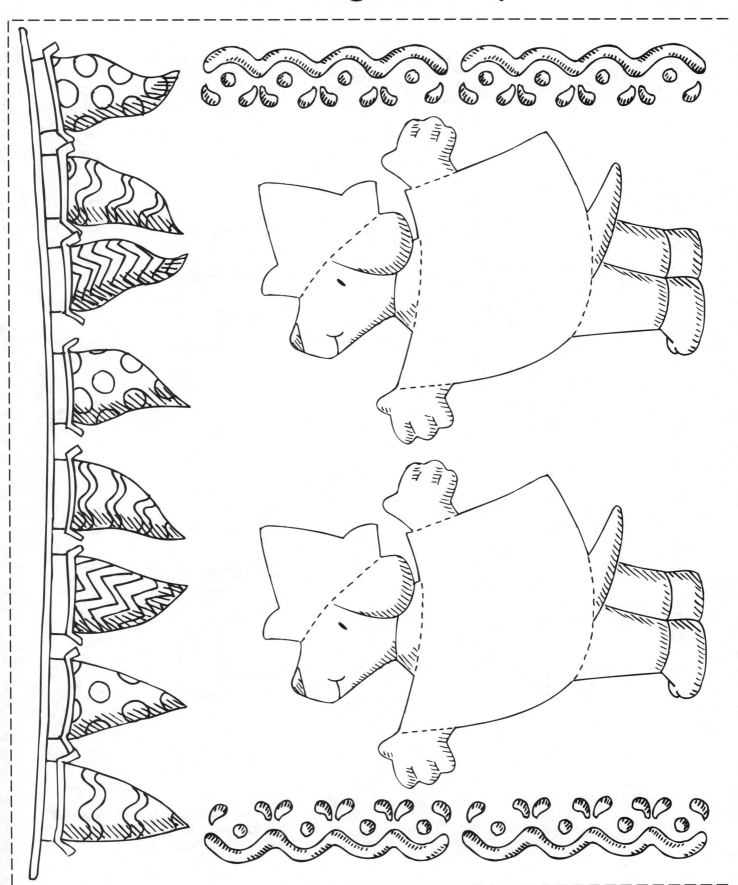

45

Circus Dogs Dress Up

Place a matching hat and cape on each circus dog.

Circus Dogs Dress Up

Reproduce, color, and cut out two sets of hats and capes.

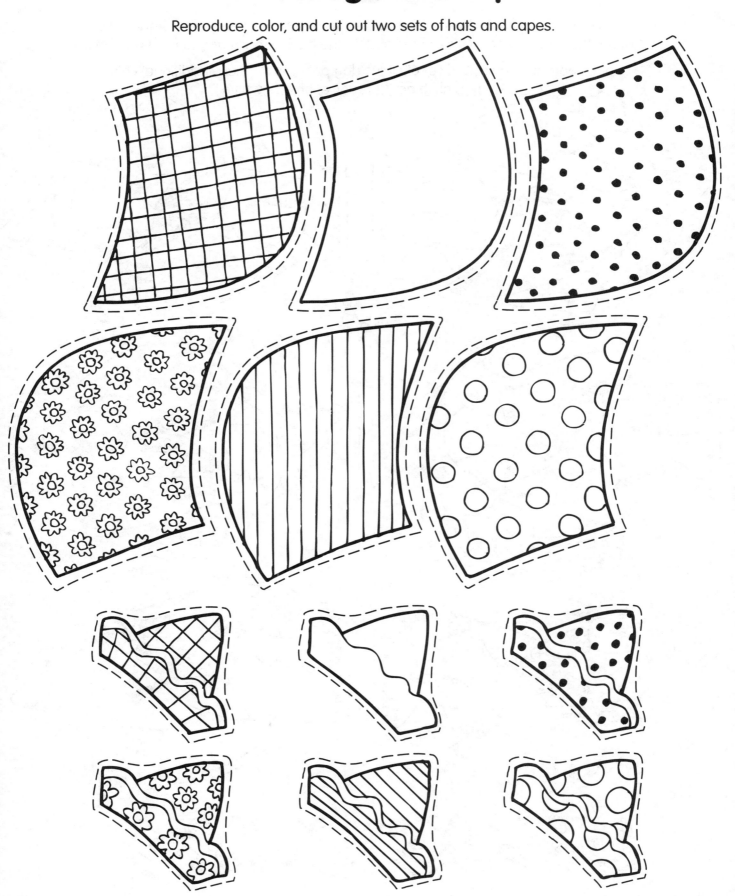

47

Circus Dog Puppets

Make It

Reproduce and color each dog a different color (red, yellow, blue, green, orange, purple). Cut out the dog patterns. Glue a craft stick to the back of each dog to form a puppet.

Note: Reproduce a second set of circus dog patterns for these additional colors (gray, pink, black, turquoise, brown, white).

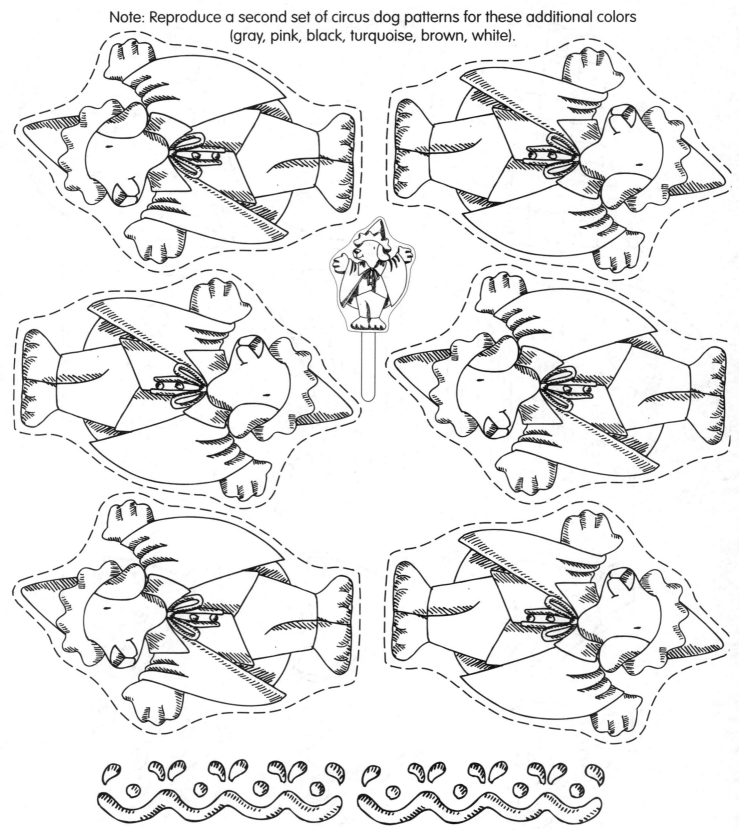

Circus Dog Labels

Reproduce, color, and cut out the labels.
Program and tape the labels on storage envelopes, boxes, folders, or drawers.

Clown in a Car

Reproduce, color, and cut out the match board.

Clown in a Car

Reproduce, color, cut out, and glue a clothespin to the back of each circle.

Clown Shapes Suit

○ Trace the shapes.
Color the picture.

Clown Shape Blocks

○ Look at each shape.
  Draw a matching shape in each block.
  Color the picture.

Clown's Shape Adventure

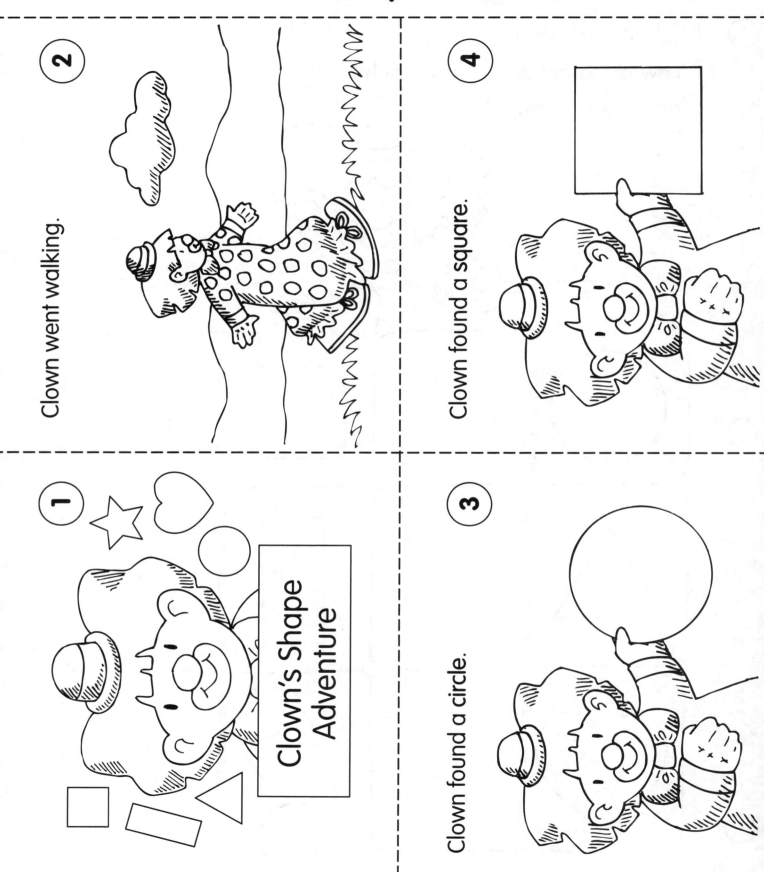

2

Clown went walking.

4

Clown found a square.

1

Clown's Shape Adventure

3

Clown found a circle.

Clown's Shape Adventure

6

Clown found a rectangle.

8

Clown found a heart.

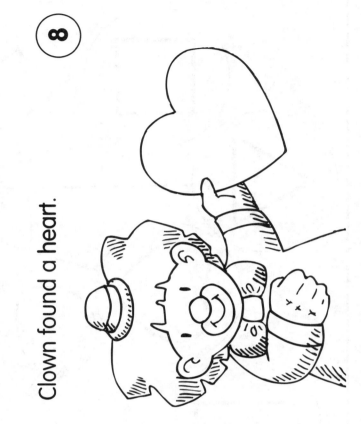

5

Clown found a triangle.

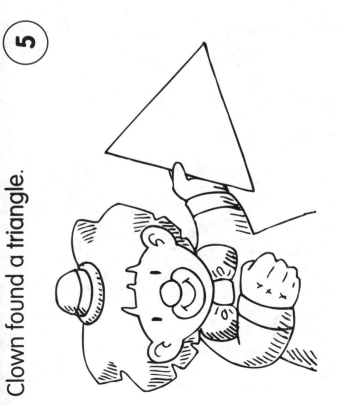

7

Clown found a star.

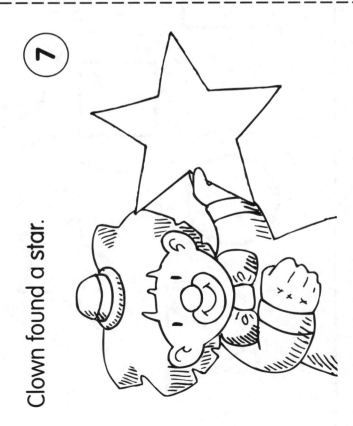

Clown's Shape Balloons

Clown's Shape Balloons

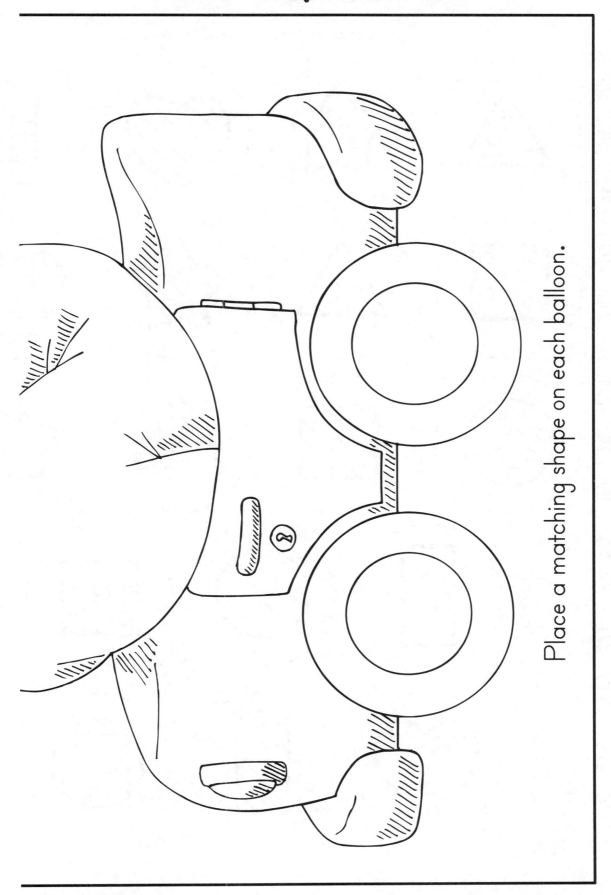

Place a matching shape on each balloon.

57

Clown's Shape Balloons

Reproduce, color, and cut out the balloons.

58

Clown Puppets

Reproduce, color, and cut out the clown patterns.
Draw a different shape on each clown's pendant (circle, square, triangle, rectangle, star, heart).
Glue a craft stick to the back of each clown to form a puppet.

Note: Reproduce a second set of clown patterns for these additional shapes
(oval, pentagon, hexagon, diamond, cone, polygon).

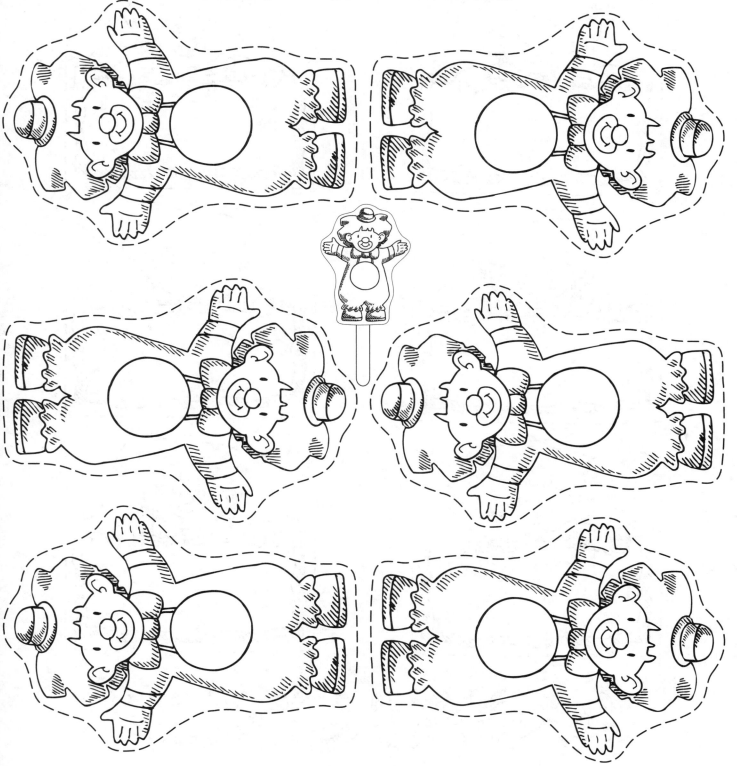

Clown Labels

Reproduce, color, and cut out the labels.
Program and tape the labels on storage envelopes, boxes, folders, or drawers.

Elephants on Parade

Reproduce, color, and cut out the match board.

61

Elephants on Parade

Reproduce, color, cut out, and glue a clothespin to the back of each elephant.

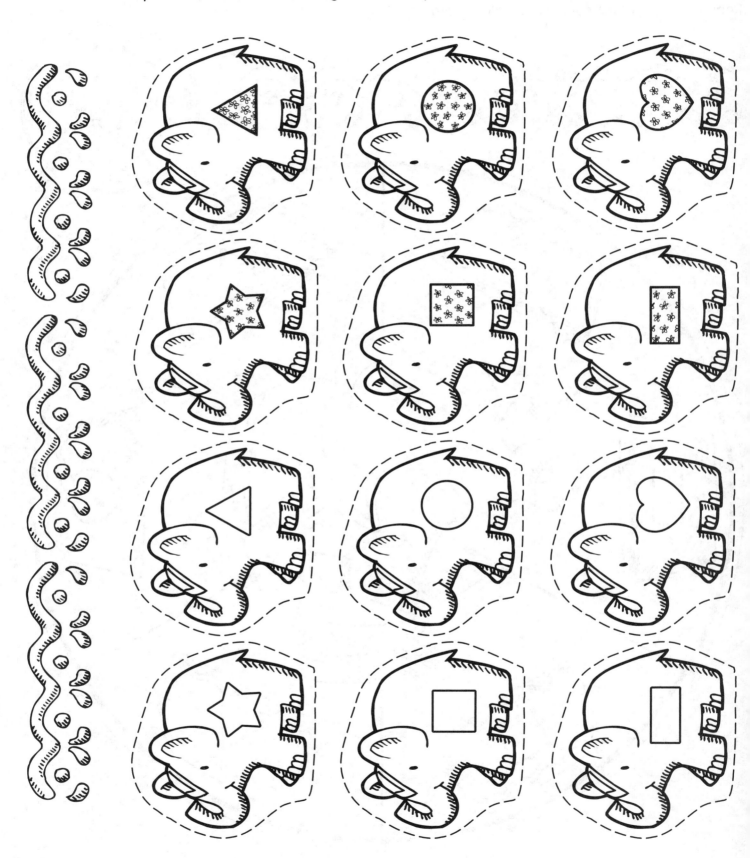

62

Balancing Elephants

○ Trace the shapes.
Color the picture.

Elephant Trunks

○ Look at the shape on each trunk.
Draw a matching shape on each trunk.
Color the picture.

64

Elephant's Shape Adventure

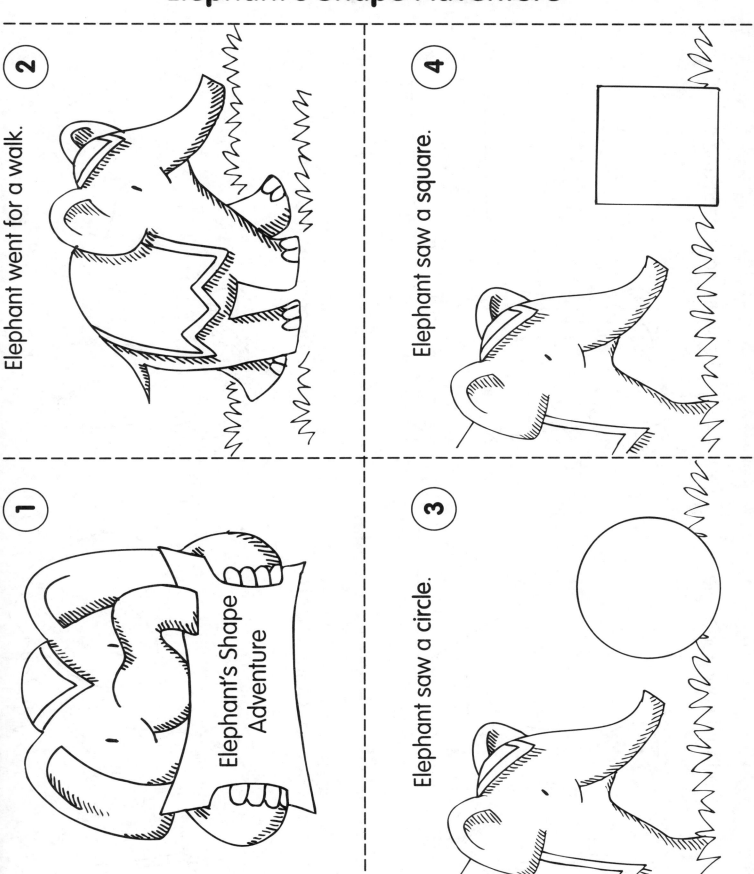

2 Elephant went for a walk.

4 Elephant saw a square.

1 Elephant's Shape Adventure

3 Elephant saw a circle.

65

Elephant's Shape Adventure

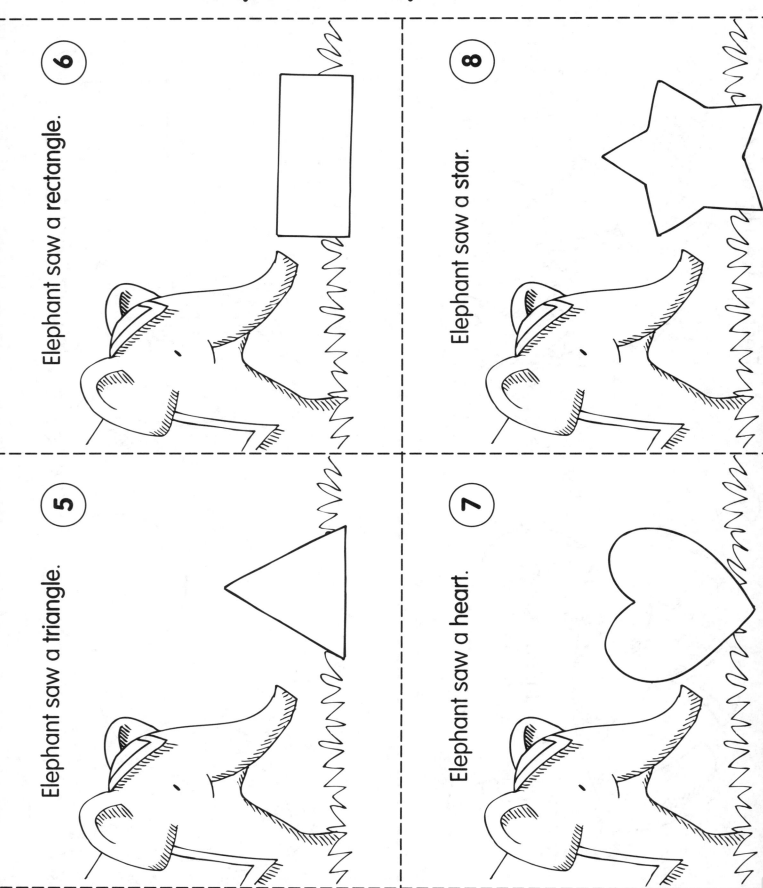

6 · Elephant saw a rectangle.

8 · Elephant saw a star.

5 · Elephant saw a triangle.

7 · Elephant saw a heart.

Elephant Quilt Match

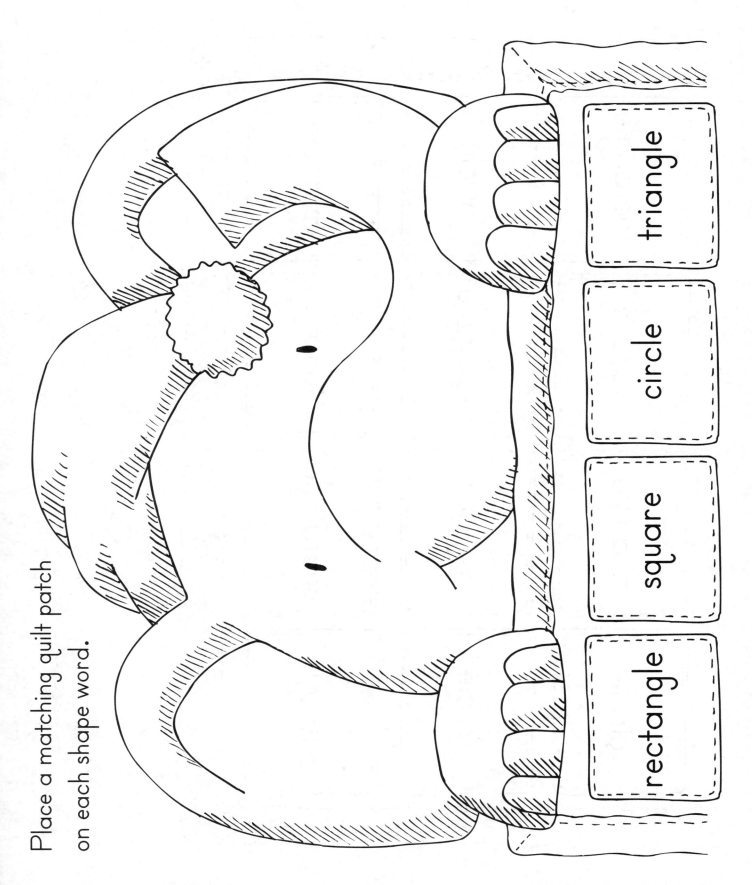

Place a matching quilt patch on each shape word.

triangle

circle

square

rectangle

67

Elephant Quilt Match

Review It

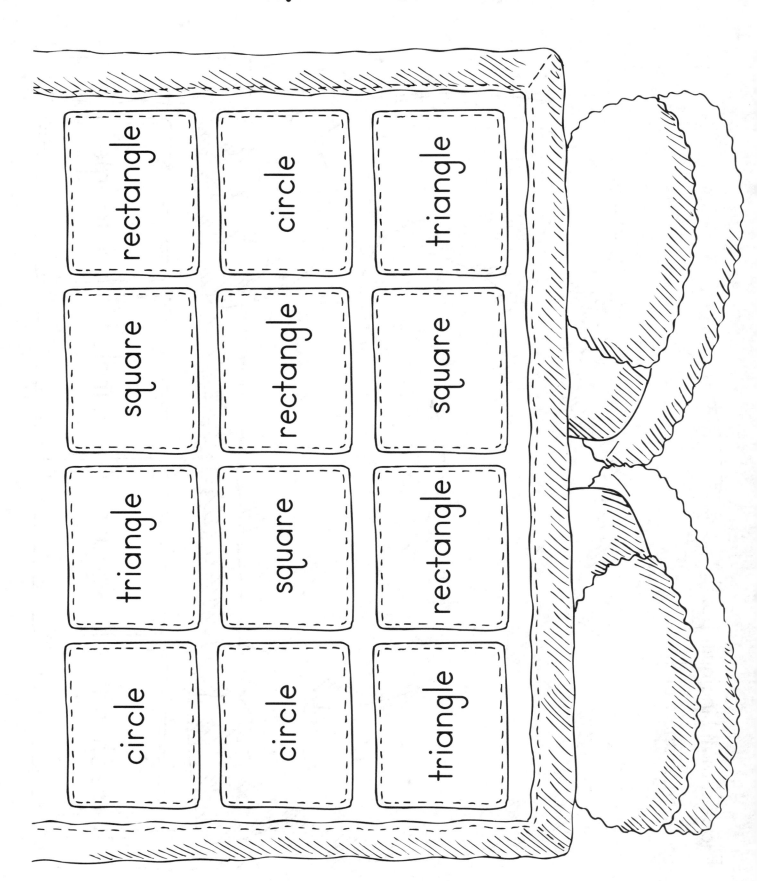

Elephant Quilt Match

Reproduce, color, and cut out the quilt squares.

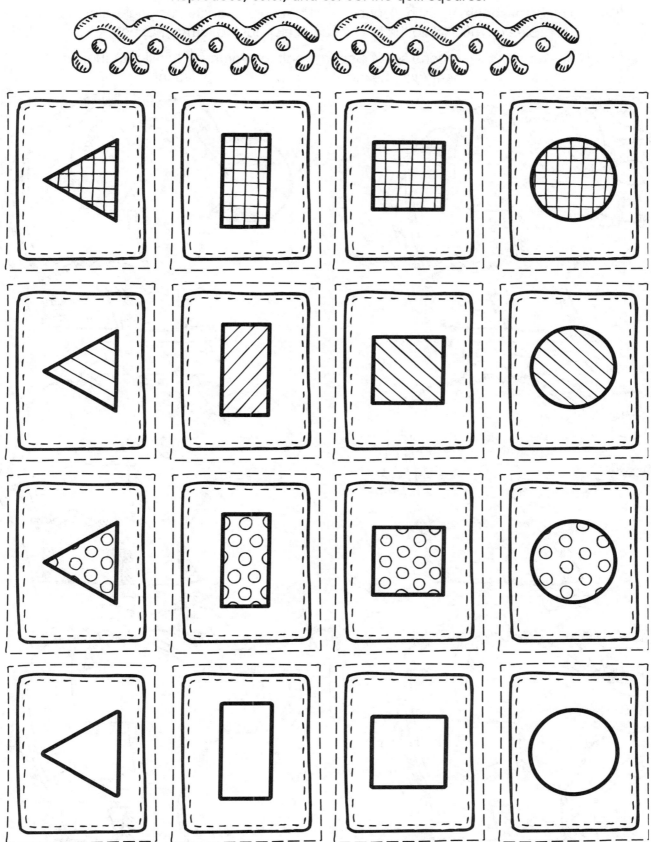

69

Elephant Puppets

Reproduce, color, and cut out the elephant patterns.
Draw a different shape on each elephant (circle, square, triangle, rectangle, star, heart).
Glue a craft stick to the back of each elephant to form a puppet.

Note: Reproduce a second set of elephant patterns for these additional shapes
(oval, pentagon, hexagon, diamond, cone, polygon).

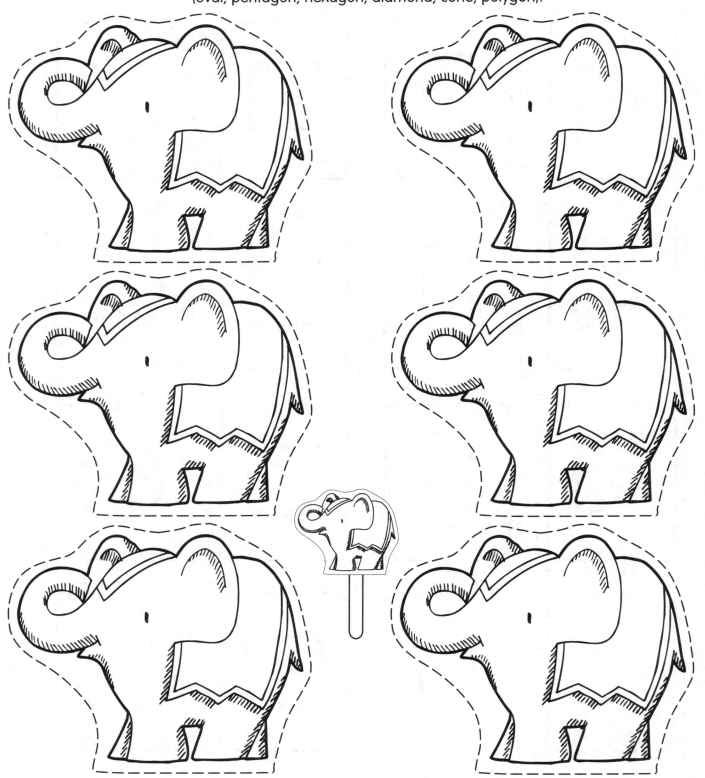

Elephant Labels

Reproduce, color, and cut out the labels.
Program and tape the labels on storage envelopes, boxes, folders, or drawers.

71

Circus Cats on Parade

Reproduce, color, and cut out the match board.

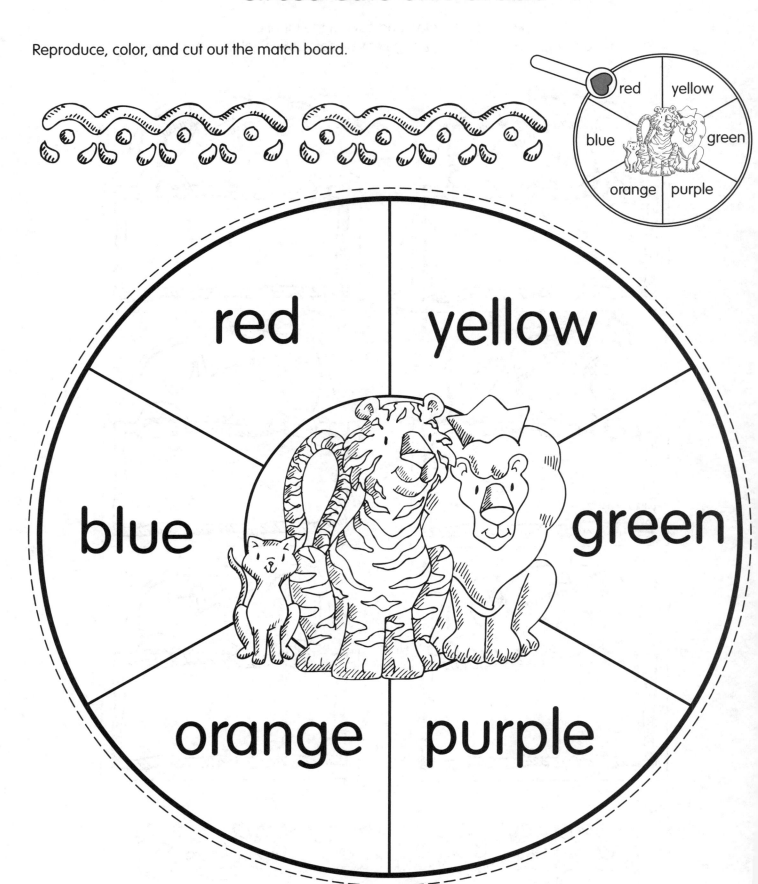

Circus Cats on Parade

Reproduce and color each set of shapes a different color (red, blue, yellow, orange, green, purple). Cut out and glue a clothespin to the back of each shape circle.

73

Acrobat Cats

○ Trace the shapes.

Color the tiger orange. Color the lion yellow.

Color the cat purple.

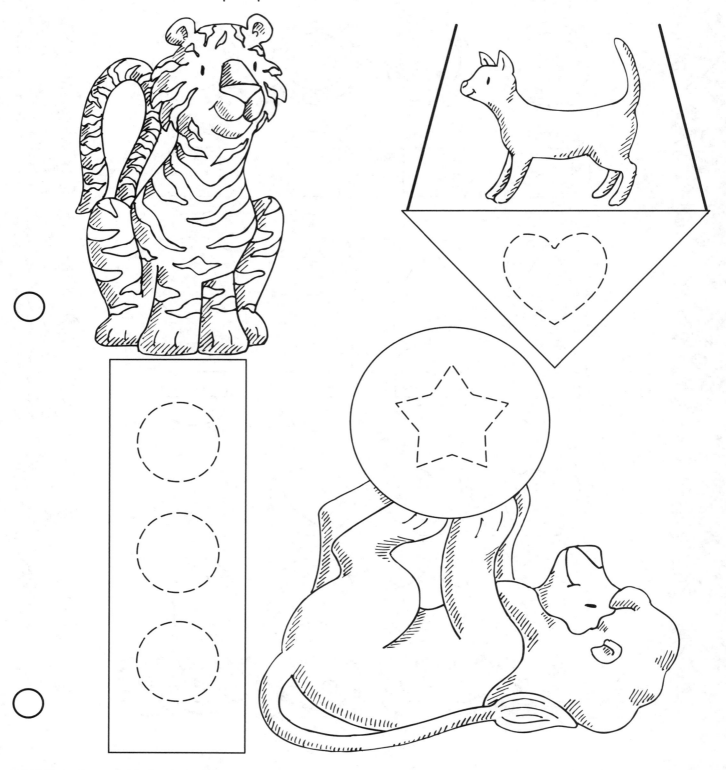

Come See the Big Cats

Look at the color legend. Color the shapes.

75

Big Cat's Color Adventure

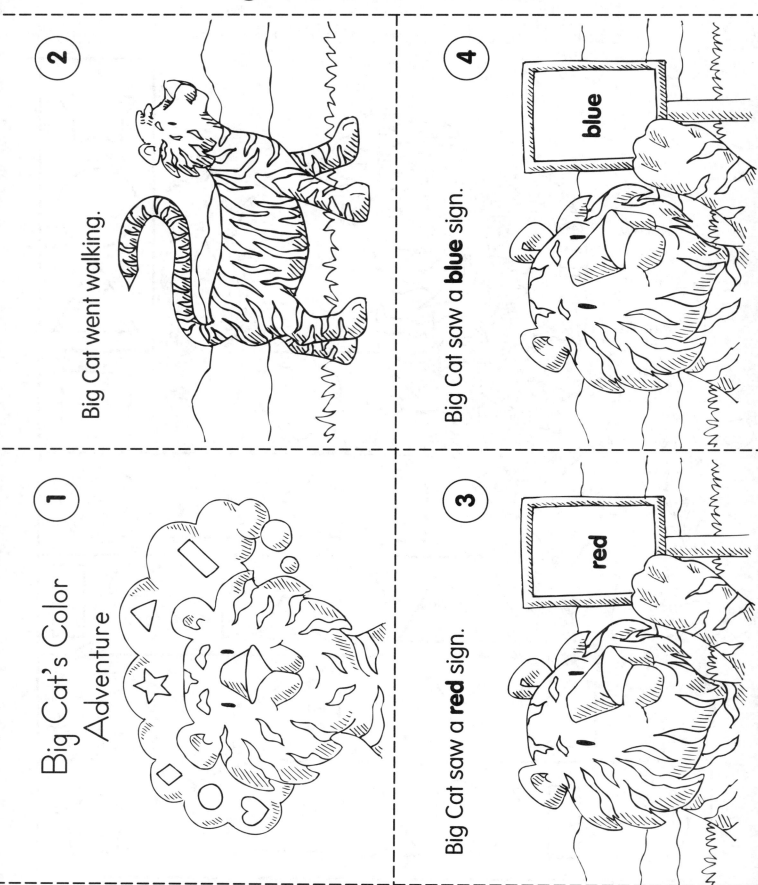

② Big Cat went walking.

④ Big Cat saw a **blue** sign.

blue

① Big Cat's Color Adventure

③ Big Cat saw a **red** sign.

red

76

6

Big Cat saw an **orange** sign.

orange

8

Big Cat saw a **purple** sign.

purple

5

Big Cat saw a **yellow** sign.

yellow

7

Big Cat saw a **green** sign.

green

Jumping Through Hoops

Place a matching color word circle on each shape.

Jumping Through Hoops

Color the shapes on each hoop a different color (red, blue, yellow, orange, green, purple).

79

Jumping Through Hoops

Reproduce, color, and cut out the circles for early learners.
Reproduce and cut out oak tag word circles for advanced learners. Do not color.

red red red

blue blue blue

yellow yellow yellow

orange orange orange

green green green

purple purple purple

Circus Cat Puppets

Reproduce, color, and cut out the tiger patterns.
Draw a different shape on each tiger's pendant (circle, square, triangle, rectangle, star, heart).
Glue a craft stick to the back of each tiger to form a puppet.

Note: Reproduce a second set of tiger patterns for additional shapes
(oval, pentagon, hexagon, diamond, cone, polygon).

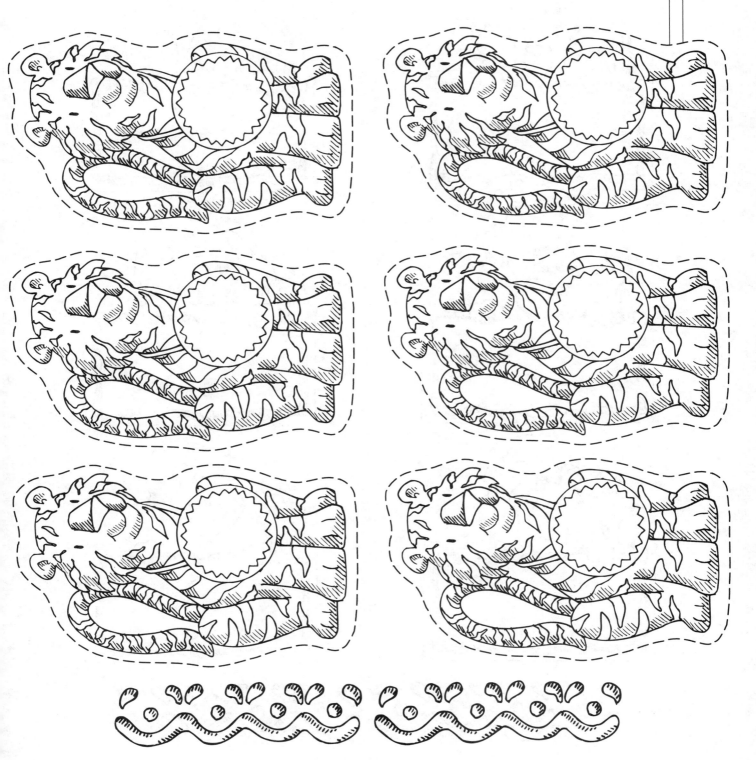

Circus Cat Labels

Reproduce, color, and cut out the labels.
Program and tape the labels on storage envelopes, boxes, folders, or drawers.

Here Comes the Circus Train

Reproduce, color, and cut out the match board.

Here Comes the Circus Train

Reproduce, color, cut out, and glue a clothespin to the back of each train.

84

Circus Cargo

○ Trace the shapes.
Color the picture.

MM2224 • *Centers for Colors & Shapes*   ©2007 Monday Morning Books, Inc.

Magic Rabbits

○ Look at each shape.

Draw a matching shape on each hat.

Color the picture.

2

What will rabbit find in the magic hat?

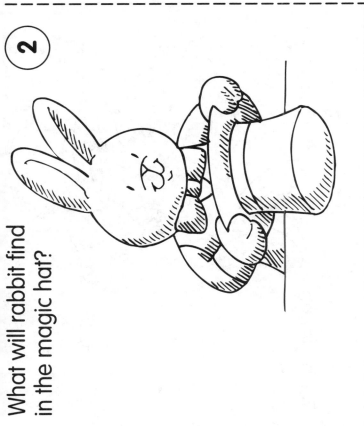

1

What's in Rabbit's Magic Hat?

4

Rabbit found a **square**.

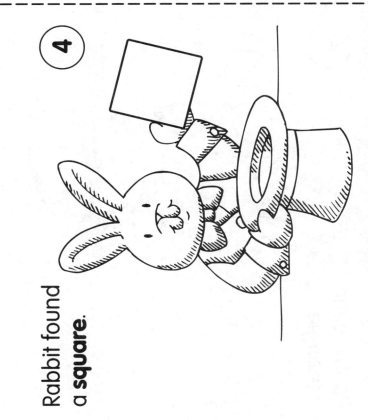

3

Rabbit found a **circle**.

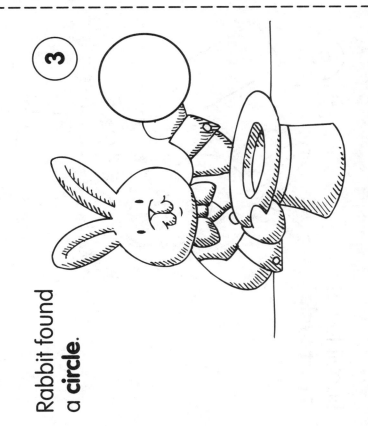

What's in Rabbit's Hat?

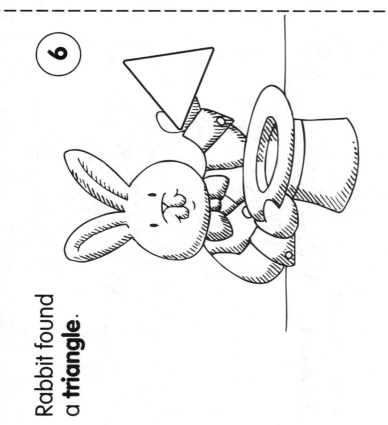

6

Rabbit found a **triangle**.

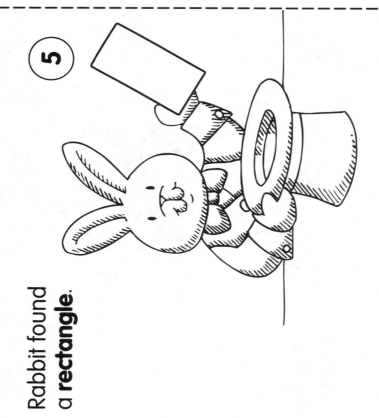

5

Rabbit found a **rectangle**.

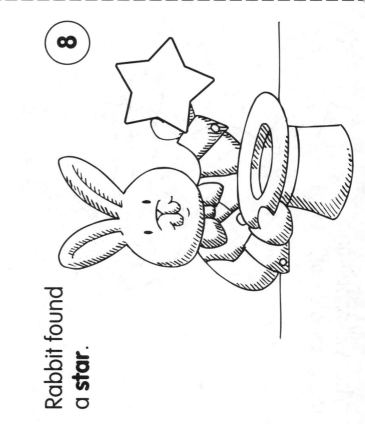

8

Rabbit found a **star**.

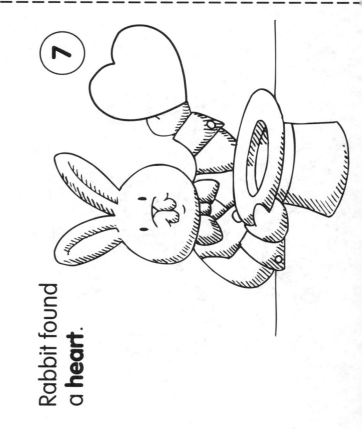

7

Rabbit found a **heart**.

... And In This Ring

89

... And In This Ring

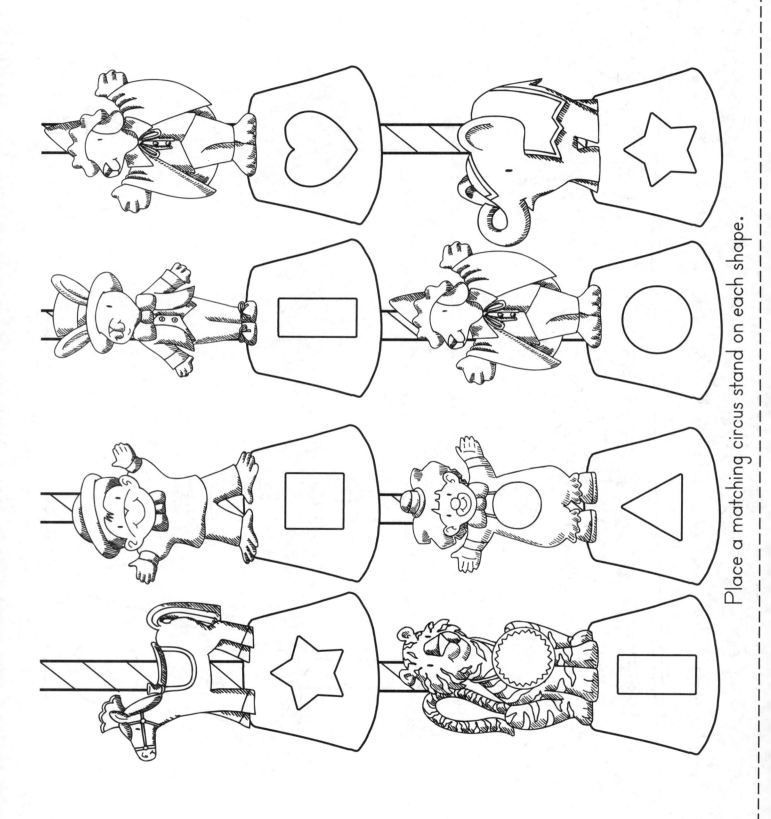

Place a matching circus stand on each shape.

90

... And In This Ring

Reproduce, color, and cut out the circus stands.

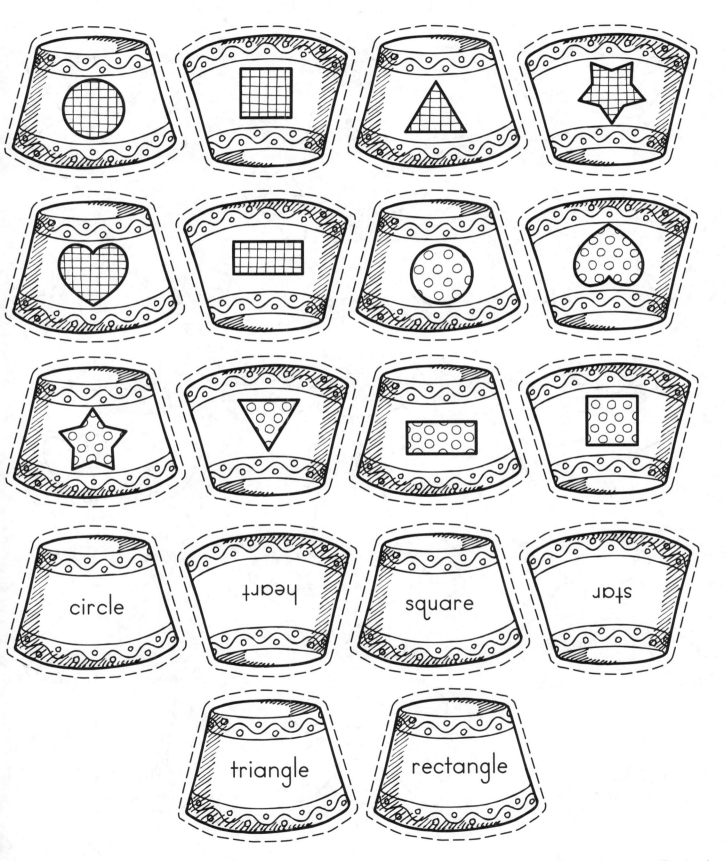

91

Magic Rabbit Puppets

Reproduce, color, and cut out the rabbit patterns.
Glue a craft stick to the back of each rabbit to form a puppet.

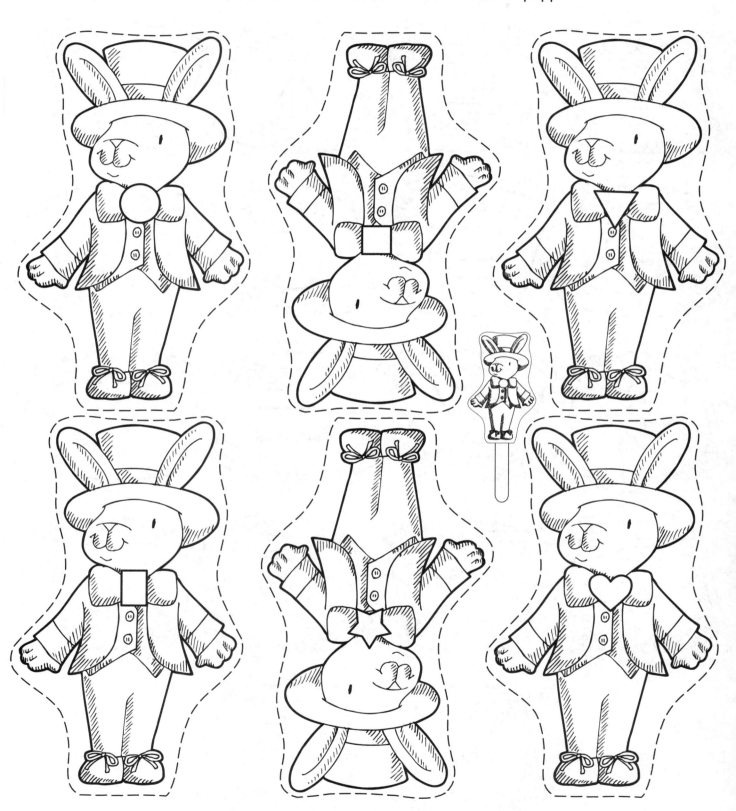

92

Rabbit Labels

Reproduce, color, and cut out the labels.
Program and tape the labels on storage envelopes, boxes, folders, or drawers.

Color or Shape of the Day Flip Chart Cover

Color or Shape of the Day
Flip Chart

Color or Shape of the Day Flip Chart Page

Borders

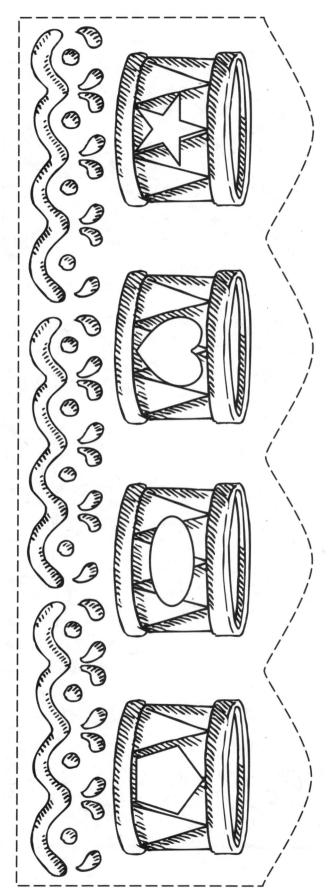

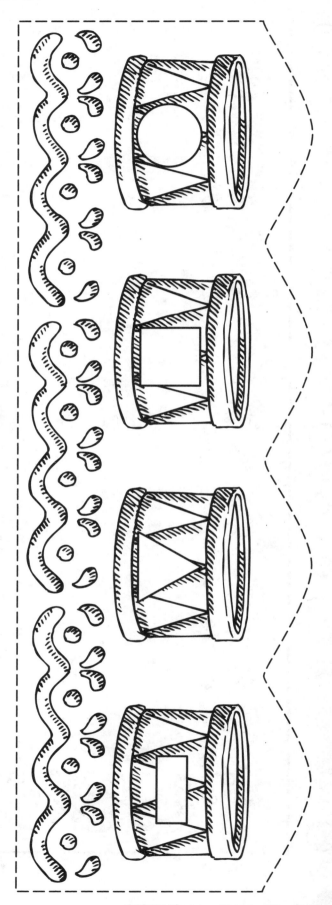

Reproduce, color, and cut out border strips to attach to folders and displays. Color each drum a different color.